YOU KNOW
A TELLY ADDICT

Emma Burgess

SUMMERSDALE

Copyright © Summersdale 2001

All rights reserved

No part of this book may be reproduced by any means, nor transmitted, nor translated into a machine language without the written permission of the publisher

Summersdale Publishers Ltd
46 West Street
Chichester
PO19 1RP

www.summersdale.com

ISBN 1 84024 177 2

Printed and bound in Great Britain

Text by Emma Burgess
Cartoons by Kate Taylor

You know you're a telly addict when...

You've seen so much *Casualty* and *ER*, you could perform open-heart surgery – whilst having an affair with one of the nurses.

YOU KNOW YOU'RE A TELLY ADDICT WHEN . . .

Whilst making love with
your partner, you cry out
Pat Butcher's name by
mistake. Whoops.

You don't bother to
decorate your house
because you're banking on
Carol Smillie and her
Changing Rooms chums doing
it for free.

The only recipe book in your
kitchen is a collection
of TV dinners.

You leave your curtains
closed so that the sun
needn't shine on your TV
screen. Sorry, that should
be plural – screens.

You know more about the cast of *Coronation Street* than the producer does.

You tell people that your bloodshot eyes are from partying too much. This is classic "denial".

You experience 'cold turkey'
if you are away from the
telly for more than a couple
of hours.

Friends tell you to
'get a life'
and they mean it.

You want to move to Albert
Square because you're
worried there isn't enough
domestic drama and crime
where you live.

15

Your life would be meaningless without television. During power cuts you are happy to stare at the blank screen.

You only learnt to read so
you could enjoy subtitled
programmes too.

You have a tattoo of the
ITV logo.

YOU KNOW YOU'RE A TELLY ADDICT WHEN . . .

You throw out your microwave to make room for a TV in the kitchen.

You suffer from RSI in your
remote control-operating
hand.

T.V.
'A reason
to live'.

You can't remember when you last saw daylight – except on TV of course.

T.V.
'A reason to live.'

The numbers on your remote are worn away from over-use, but that's fine because you know them by touch.

23

You hide your stash of TV
guides underneath your
dirty magazines.

You fund research into
Braille TV – in case your
other big addiction really
does cause blindness.

You find out what day it is
by watching the News.

You make a hefty annual income from all your *You've Been Framed* entries.

27

Your doorbell rings the opening bar of the *Neighbours* theme.

YOU KNOW YOU'RE A TELLY ADDICT WHEN . . .

YOU KNOW YOU'RE A TELLY ADDICT WHEN . . .

And your mobile ringer sounds suspiciously like the song from *Friends*.

You still insist on sleeping
with your *Simpsons*
matching duvet and
pillowcase set.

In fact, most of your belongings are TV show merchandise.

T.V.
'A reason
to live'.

YOU KNOW YOU'RE A TELLY ADDICT WHEN . . .

YOU KNOW YOU'RE A TELLY ADDICT WHEN . . .

The only CDs you own are
TV theme compilations.

You're saving up for plastic surgery. You'll be the first human with a TellyTubby-style 'monitor implant' to the abdomen.

35

When people ask you what your friends are called, you say 'Jennifer Aniston, Lisa Kudrow, David Schwimmer and the other guys'.

Your partner leaves you,
citing a soap opera
character in the divorce.

You've replaced pictures of
your mum, dad and siblings
with photos of *The Waltons*.
They're your family now.

After a course of regressional hypnosis, you're not surprised to learn that you were one of *The Flintstones* in a past life.

You're the only person who
longs for the return of
the Test Card.

41

YOU KNOW YOU'RE A TELLY ADDICT WHEN . . .

You're convinced you
shot J.R.

You've unwittingly qualified
for several Open University
degrees simply by never
turning the TV off at night.

T.V.
'A reason
to live'.

YOU KNOW YOU'RE A TELLY ADDICT WHEN . . .

The only books you own are TV scripts. Not that you read them – you know every episode of *Blackadder* word for word.

T.V.
'A reason to live'.

You count channels,
    not sheep.

You know the names of every VT editor, gaffer and dolly grip. And you understand what they actually do.

T.V. 'A reason to live.'

You stop to take down every
PO Box address offered at
the end of programmes, no
matter how irrelevant.
These are the only contact
details in your
address book.

You've recently
commissioned a bust of
John Logie Baird – the great
inventor of television.

You're up and dressed at 7am just in case *The Big Breakfast* crew comes knocking at your door.

Your optician was forced to
carry out pioneering surgery
to round off your
square eyes.

YOU KNOW YOU'RE A TELLY ADDICT WHEN . . .

You know weather
presenters' names.

53

You might not regard
yourself as a 'couch potato',
but if you ever breed you'll
probably spawn a pound of
King Edwards.

T.V.
'A reason
to live'.

55

You've been banned from appearing on Noel Edmonds' show *Telly Addicts* because you take the title of the show literally.

T.V.
'A reason
to live'.

You're the first person to have set up an annual standing order for your TV licence and to think that it's good value for money.

You always win the
'entertainment' section in
general knowledge quizzes.

58

You had a breakdown when
Thames lost its franchise
for ITV.

You learn the TV listings off
by heart each morning.

YOU KNOW YOU'RE A TELLY ADDICT WHEN . . .

You have several TV monitors in your living room so that you can watch all the channels at once.

T.V. 'A reason to live.'

When you're not glued to the box, you're online. The Beeb has a great website.

T.V.
'A reason
to live'.

If the TV scheduling isn't up
to scratch, at least you have
your PlayStation to
fall back on.

63

Lara Croft is real to you.

Your ambition is to take part in enough game shows from which to earn a living.

T.V.
'A reason to live'.

65

TV researchers nationwide
have your number, and
they're the only ones who
ever call.

The home videos you make
comprise shots of you
watching TV.

You've been in the audience of so many TV talk shows that Esther, Trisha and Kilroy would all recognise you in the street. And avoid you.

When out shopping you're
transfixed by
in-store cameras.

69

You don't see the point of
going abroad when you can
enjoy vicarious holidays with
the *Wish You Were
Here* team.

T.V.
'A reason
to live'.

When Channel Four celebrated its 10th anniversary, you too had a party. On your own.

T.V.
'A reason
to live'.

YOU KNOW YOU'RE
A TELLY ADDICT WHEN . . .

Your ideal job would be
working in Radio Rentals.

You can name every *Top of the Pops* presenter ever – in chronological order.

As a baby, you learnt to
switch channels before you
could walk or talk.

75

YOU KNOW YOU'RE A TELLY ADDICT WHEN . . .

You were probably the only
person that didn't feel sorry
for Jim Carrey's character
in *The Truman Show*.

You contain more TV trivia
than a *Trivial Pursuit*
warehouse.

You've disowned your own
parents and written to
Richard and Judy, asking
them to adopt you.
Still no response.

You never miss the Queen's
Christmas Speech.

You get upset if people talk
when the credits are
still rolling.

You know the answers to all
the big questions: What's
the meaning of life? TV,
of course.

You've learnt most of the
current affairs you know
from watching *Panorama*.

T.V.
'A reason
to live'.

YOU KNOW YOU'RE A TELLY ADDICT WHEN . . .

As a kid you tried to persuade your parents to take you away from school, claiming everything you'll ever need to know can be gleaned from *Blue Peter*.

T.V.
'A reason to live'.

You've been short-listed as
a potential BBC
Programme Controller.

TV Chiefs are deeply
grateful to obsessive people
like you – if a little scared.

You took up smoking to help
beat your telly addiction.
Then drink.

YOU KNOW YOU'RE A TELLY ADDICT WHEN . . .

A romantic night in bed with
your partner is spent
watching your own
separate TVs.

Your doctor has prescribed
pills for the panic attacks
you experience when there's
transmission interference
on your television.

You cry with genuine pity at
learning that some people
don't own a television.

You're the only person of
your generation to watch
Songs of Praise, and dare I
say it, sing along.

YOU KNOW YOU'RE A TELLY ADDICT WHEN . . .

You wear 3-d glasses round your neck in the same way that normal people would wear their reading glasses.

YOU KNOW YOU'RE A TELLY ADDICT WHEN . . .

So does your dog.

You actually know what ALL
the buttons on a remote
controller are for.

Sesame Street taught you
how to count and how to
negotiate your way through
the alphabet. (You must be
the only person in this
country to 'thank
the letter zee'.)

You were one of the first
people to notice when the
Eastenders opening
sequence incorporated The
Dome in its bird's eye view
of the River Thames.

100

Your partner suspects you
learnt your sexual habits
from watching too many
wildlife programmes.

You nominated Noel
Edmonds for Mayor
of London.

T.V.
'A reason
to live'

YOU KNOW YOU'RE
A TELLY ADDICT WHEN . . .

NOEL
EDMONDS
FOR
MAYOR

103

You need therapy, but Raj Persaud and that other agony aunt from *This Morning* will do.

T.V.
'A reason to live'.

YOU KNOW YOU'RE A TELLY ADDICT WHEN . . .

You have a huge phone-bill.
This isn't testimony to your
scores of friends, but your
love of TV phone-ins.

T.V.
'A reason
to live'.

You have applied for
American Citizenship.
Actually you can't stand
Americans, but they do have
a greater richness in variety
when in comes to
TV channels.

106

You know the colour of
Denis Norden's clipboard.

T.V.
'A reason
to live'.

YOU KNOW YOU'RE A TELLY ADDICT WHEN . . .

You find it hard to talk to people without an autocue.

You know more about Sky
than Rupert Murdoch.

You get the all the newspapers delivered to your house daily. Well, just the TV guide pullouts.

YOU KNOW YOU'RE A TELLY ADDICT WHEN . . .

You install video cameras all over your house to record your own inaction.

You tolerate Mr Blobby.

Likewise Mr Bean.

You don't despair when your
lover dumps you, as you
know you'll find love in the
next episode.

T.V.
'A reason
to live'

114

Like most addicts, you've
been in denial for a
long time.

You even remember the
pilot programmes that
weren't good enough to
make into series.

YOU KNOW YOU'RE A TELLY ADDICT WHEN . . .

You are socially inept.

T.V.
'A reason to live'.

You want to end your life on
a real cliff-hanger, like
most good dramas.

Paradoxically, you're quite
entertaining. You should be
in a Freak Show.

If you were a little bit more
charismatic, you still
wouldn't have any charisma.

You'd rather watch *Blind Date* than go on one.

YOU KNOW YOU'RE A TELLY ADDICT WHEN . . .

You schedule your daughter's wedding around the TV listings.

You're insulted when people call you a 'nerd'. After all, it's not as if you spend all day on a computer. That would be nerdy.

You recognise the names of
the Radio Times editors.

T.V.
'A reason
to live.'

You learnt how to drive
from watching 'Top Gear'.
No wonder you still haven't
passed your test.

Your idea of a good
bedtime read is Ceefax –
especially page 100.

**For the latest humour books
from Summersdale, check out**

www.summersdale.com